child
of a stolen
homeland

Karim Wafa

First published in 2024

First edition 2024

This paperback edition has been published in 2024

ISBN: 978-99901-97-07-5

for Palestine,
the land of my ancestors
the cradle of the three religions:
Judaism, Christianity, and Islam

Karim Wafa

note

almost all of my poems are in lowercase
letters because i honor Arabic, my native
language, which does not have any capital
letters, and also because i personally prefer
the look of it as it seems like all words are
equally flowing from one line to the next.

the only words in my poems that escape this
rule are those referring to official names of
places or to God, the latter of which being a
form of respect for the Divine.

child of a stolen homeland

they ignore the suffering of millions
saying they do not understand it
but i ask them:
in what language does a child cry?

child of a stolen homeland

i was just a kid
the first time i was told
that my people were shadows
cast aside by the world
for existing on a piece of land
the world was obsessed with
so we paid the price
but they do not realize
that whatever happens
we are here
and always will be

Karim Wafa

i looked up to the sky

expecting to see a clear blue ocean above

but it was dark and grey

not from the weather or maybe even a storm

but from the fumes of far-flung bombs

dropped over our heads like rain drops

but unlike rain drops

those bombs did not bring life

they instead brought the very opposite

and the world sat by and watched

us being removed from the earth

one by one

child of a stolen homeland

dear homeland of my ancestors,

i miss you

it's been a long time since we spoke

my grandma always tells me stories

about how your air is the cleanest

your waters the freshest

and your people the nicest

i no longer know what to say

you've been betrayed by the world

and what's worse

is that they blame you for suffering

they want you to stay quiet and never speak

time will reveal their true colors

in the end i know we will be victorious

and i'll be able to place my hand on your

soil

kiss the graves of my elders

and bow down

to the holy shrine of the blessed city

but until that day comes

i'm still a lost soul in exile

betrayed by the world

just like you

maybe if the colour of my skin was lighter

or my features a bit finer

the world would have saved me and my

people

but we are too ethnic for this world

too indigenous

too ancient

too authentic

that is what they are trying to erase

our history

child of a stolen homeland

they do not hear our screams
because they have been tricked into
believing
that our suffering is from a faraway land
and therefore incomprehensible
unable to understand the language of our
cries
but they forget
that we share one common language
and that is humanity

my grandmother points to the television

screen

she tells me

"look ya habibi

this is where i grew up"

i sadly do not know this place

because my soul is a stranger

to the land of my ancestors

her eyes fill with tears

"it used to be so beautiful"

her voice breaks and she starts weeping

i can see a tear

drop onto her embroidered tribal dress

the same dress that one can no longer find

because my homeland has been stolen

and my culture erased

child of a stolen homeland

i close my eyes

and my soul gets torn apart

i wonder how the world was okay

with watching us suffer

then i understand

that they do not see us as people

not even animals

or flowers

or plants

they think we are worthless

our colour

our language

our tribes

our religions

to them we are nothing

and that is what made it so easy

to eradicate our nation

i don't understand

how they constantly talk

about humanity and equality

but denying it to us

when we fight

for these same principles

do they not see the double standards?

do they not see the hypocrisy?

do they not see the lies?

it's like talking to a wall

we are tired

i am tired

child of a stolen homeland

i remember the voices of the children from
my village
so pure and angelic they were
now they are with the angels
and they have even turned into them
taken from this world
far too soon

we are native people

what we are going through

our brothers and sisters

on the other side of the ocean

also experienced

centuries ago

from turtle island

to my people in the holy land

from the islands of the sea

we are the nomads

the bedouins

the tribesmen

the warriors

we are living and breathing nature

they know they have no connection to it

and that is why they are jealous

of our ancestral power

we will forever live on

in the rivers, streams, winds, and soil

because we are native

child of a stolen homeland

and the native soul goes back to nature
just as he was created from it

i could hear the lullabies of my people
the voices of my ancestors in nature
since our land was taken i only hear cries
from a world far away
but also very near
they said that our land was empty
with no people or culture
what they did not tell you
was that our people have been here
since the beginning of time

people say columbus discovered their land

and that the british empire discovered ours

none of them discovered anything

my people and my cousins

on the other side of the ocean

we have been here since man has been on

the earth

but because we do not look

like the oppressor

they said our lands were empty

because to them we were not people

child of a stolen homeland

my people

have a right

to live

just like

anybody else

and the fact

that the world

does not see this

is beyond me

Karim Wafa

i can hear the voices of my ancestors

when i pick olives

during the autumn harvest

but the settler burnt my olive trees

now i can no longer

speak to my elders

child of a stolen homeland

can they say that we matter?
when they witness our suffering
observe our alienation
and watch our extermination
without batting an eye?

one day our land will be free

and i'll be able to walk on the farms of my

elders

i'll be able to sit under an olive tree

shaded from the blistering sun

i'll be able to speak my own language

without being called a threat

i'll be unapologetically indigenous

on my native land

and those are

my ancestor's wildest dreams

they think that we are less valuable

because of the way we look

the language we speak

the religions we follow

the heritage we carry

they do not realize

that the real inferior one

is the one who sees himself

as superior to others

one day when the sun will shine

all flowers will bloom

all people will rejoice

and fear of oppression will be gone

i can't wait

for that day to come

child of a stolen homeland

how can they claim to bring peace?
when in reality their mere presence
has caused peace to flee from our land
and turn into a refugee

Karim Wafa

we wake up and cry
we go to sleep and cry
we are a nation that cries
just as much as it breathes

child of a stolen homeland

i am trying to understand

how peaceful people

overnight turned into monsters

people who were supposedly

on the side of peace

suddenly endorsed violence

if the trees could speak

they would scream

the names of my elders

to come and save them

and they would tell you all

that the angels

the world has been worshiping

were actually nothing short of demons

eventually the truth will be out there

and the world will know

that it has been lied to

this entire time

child of a stolen homeland

do they not see themselves?
pretending to bring peace
when the only thing they bring
is destruction and gloom

no matter how much

land they take

farms they burn

rivers they poison

or cities are built

on top of all this destruction

they will never have peace

because their souls

will forever be tormented

by the evilness of their ways

child of a stolen homeland

the more i see of this world

i realize that honest souls are tormented

while dishonest ones are rewarded

the rules of society

are against everything we have learnt

that is when i understood

that this world

is not made for the believers

i know that this world is a joke

it is ruled by monsters

void of any emotions and humanity

at this point

i'd rather settle for a fantasy

child of a stolen homeland

how much longer can this go on?
innocent lives lost
all for the greed
of a select few

they will never be at peace
as long as they continue destroying
instead of nurturing

child of a stolen homeland

my village was full of life

now it is full of grief

i just wish

all those souls could come back

you were at home

they destroyed it

you went to school

they destroyed it

you went to the hospital

they destroyed it

as your last option

you went to your house of worship

to be with God

but they destroyed it

and they call themselves

the children of the Lord

please tell me

which Lord do they speak of?

whatever they build

on our stolen land

is destined to crumble

as it will suffer the wrath

of the souls of our nation

who are no longer in this world

because the oppressor wanted

all that we had

Karim Wafa

our homeland

used to be the garden of life

now it is a graveyard

giving out tickets

to departed souls

child of a stolen homeland

we will never give up
our ancestors did not
so why should we?

people around the world

are allowed to breathe and to thrive

except for mine

my people cry for every waking hour

and struggle to survive

even in the night

taking a simple breath

becomes an act of resistance

in the eyes of the oppressor

as he can never allow us

to survive or live

let alone thrive

the truth we embody

threatens the establishment of lies

that they have created

on the corpses of our elders

taken from this world because

they were the keepers of knowledge

purposely done

to keep the world plagued by ignorance

child of a stolen homeland

when will this world understand

that it rests on the pillars of oppression

that have been concealed

behind a veil of sweetened lies

to keep you ignorant

about the things you ought to know

you are in a daze

fuelled by a form of timeless oppression

while people around the world

carry designer bags

in an act of competition

people in my land

carry the broken parts

of their loved ones,

that's oppression.

young people from all over

stuff their faces with ravishing delights

those from my barren nation

struggle to find a loaf of bread to feed a

dozen

they say the 21st century is a blessing

as it brings people together once and for all.

when it comes to my people

you watched us being wiped out before

your eyes

only confining us to the dusty pages

of an old forgotten history.

child of a stolen homeland

tell me why

children around the world

enjoy the beauty of their youth

ravishing in the marvels of every new day

while the children of my land

pray for an ending to this cursed oppression

people call existence

wishing they were in the gardens of

paradise

as it is the only place they can see their

families

to eat and drink in peace

they pray for the afterlife

because this one

has been a nightmare

they ask kids around the world

what the morning sounds like

and they say "birds chirping"

kids in my land have a different answer

when asked the same question

they reply with "explosions"

kids around the world say that the night

is quiet except for the faint sound of

crickets

whereas those of my land say "explosions"

once more

they ask those same kids what they dream

of

and they answer "friends, family and fun"

but when the children of my land are asked

they answer "how can we dream?

we never have

and never will

because the moment we close our eyes

we know that they will stay closed

for eternity"

young souls from the four corners of the
globe
think of how their future will look like
young souls from my land
know no such privilege
for the only thing they can think of
is if they will be lucky enough
to see the sunrise again

i have a long time ago lost hope

in the principles of equality, brotherhood

and freedom

for i know that it is nothing but a farce

people pretending to have each other's

backs

when they wound those same backs when

they turn

the only principles that guide this cruel

world

are those of selfishness, greed, and division

child of a stolen homeland

man only knows how to pronounce fancy
words

drafting agreements, constitutions, and
declarations

but they are all void of any substance

as we know far too well

that the words and letters only exist on
paper

but vanish

the moment they need to be implemented

those from this world say they want
freedom
but we know very well
that they cannot stand seeing it on all
people
in their eyes only a select few deserve it
while those of various features and hues
must have it denied
so i know the game that they play
and the next time they talk about freedom
i'll ask:
does it also apply to those who look like
me?

child of a stolen homeland

if you listen closely

you can hear the voices of my ancestors

as you walk

you can hear the beating of the drum

as your sit

you can hear their voices

gathered around a ceremonial dish

as you prepare your meal

you can hear the voices of our women

sing the ancient songs of the village farmers

and even when you go to sleep

the cracking voices of our grandparents

carry you from this world

to the realm of the ancestors

will the world forever remain silent?

as it sees its own people perishing

has humanity lost the will to feel?

it seems as if empathy no longer exists

they stay silent as they witness oppression

they claim to be civilized and developed

when they are no such thing

they are the definition of barbarism

an inhumanity taken

from the depths of hell

and brought to reality

child of a stolen homeland

i just want to close my eyes

and be told that this was all a dream

i do this

but realize i am only distracting myself

from a suffering i cannot describe

i am at a loss for words

because no words even exist

that can begin to describe this nightmare

Karim Wafa

we will never forgive the world

for their silence

as they sat by and watched

us being wiped off the earth

child of a stolen homeland

i've been lied to

i was told that all men were created equal

a statement that made me the happiest

but then reality hit

and i realized that this was all a fantasy

nothing but fancy words

aimed at keeping angry voices at bay

but there comes a time

when man must take control of his own

destiny

and let the world know

that even if the world never saw him as an

equal

he forever will be

are they not tired?

of lying to our faces

and expecting us to believe every word they

say

the idea of their inherent supremacy

is the root of all evil

for it has caused famines, conflicts, and

more

all painted in a benevolent light

while those who suffered

were seen as sub-human

and i'll never forget

how you all fell for their lies

and watched my people perish

child of a stolen homeland

can we not close our eyes

just for a second

without the fear

of never being able to open them again?

can they say

that they are all for freedom

while doing the most inhuman of things?

can they say that they value all lives

while at the same time

taking away those of people who look like

me?

can they keep on spewing these lies

while the world stays silent?

they told me that we were all one
something that put a smile on my face
but that smile quickly vanished
just as fast as they made my people vanish
erasing our culture, nation, and history
i quickly understood
that when they say they see the world as
one
what they truly mean is one versus one
they have never seen us as equals
what a fool i must have been
to think that they would think of us as
people
who was i kidding
we were nothing to them
and to see that
i just had to take a look at how history
treated us

child of a stolen homeland

figures of the western world

thrive on the suffering of the eastern one

it seems like a nightmare

instead of a reality

but the pillars of their institutions

were built on the suffering of my people

they walk about happily talking about

freedom

while denying it to people who look like me

that's when i knew

that my elders were right

about how those who claim to "come in

peace"

seek to "leave us in pieces"

do they not realize

that he who was created

from the piece of land

they are so desperate to steal

will never, ever, surrender

we are not like the others

the spirits of our elders

beat the warrior drums of our souls

every breath we take

is followed by a breath from the animals

and trees

the rivers and streams

don't they realize

they can never remove me

because i am indigenous

and if they do

i will come back in the next generation

and i will permeate through

the spirits of nature

child of a stolen homeland

the olive trees

live for almost a millennia

they have seen everything

so, when that time comes

they will testify

in favour of the native soul

who comes from the native land

i used to see the sunshine

but now even that is gone

as it is clouded by the spirits of darkness

that seek to destroy our nation

and uproot our land

but don't they realize

that i'll never leave my land

in spite of them taking away the sun

i'll resist in the dark

child of a stolen homeland

one day

the sun will shine

over my homeland

the farmer will return

to his ancestral farm

but the people will still wait

for the return of their loved ones

that is a wish

that is confined

to the realm of spirits

i walked on the land

my elders also walked on

every step i take

is followed by those of my ancestors

their names can be heard

in the gentle sound of the wind

as the breeze ruffles leaves here and there

feeling a warm embrace

in the coldest circumstances

people think i am alone

they do not know

that i'm never alone

child of a stolen homeland

my people cling onto

a piece of land

that tells a story

from a long time ago

a time forgotten by many

but not by my elders

for they see history in their mind

they hear the past in their ears

they speak words from the beyond

but they are lost in translation

as this world has traded the bitter truth

for artificially sweetened lies

leaders of the "free world"

is what they claim to be

as they deny freedom

to all people who do not look like them

i am tired

of putting my hopes

in a system that has never

seen me as an equal

child of a stolen homeland

they take the lives of thousands

if not millions

of people from my tribe, homeland and

nation

while all people stay silent

scared to anger the oppressor

do you not realize?

that he never did

and never will

see us as human beings

let me take a glimpse of my homeland

for one last time

before it is taken away from me

like my ancestors

who were ripped from their homes

and pushed to the ocean

they had no place to go

but they had a place they came from

child of a stolen homeland

how can i keep on smiling

while my people

are having their smiles taken from their

faces

with no happiness left in their body

she told him

"i'm waiting for this world

to be a happy place"

he took her hand

squeezed it tight

and said

"my love...

it has always been a happy place

humans are at fault...

...for making it a living hell"

child of a stolen homeland

maybe all of this has just been a dream
and sometimes kind of a nightmare
where i can't wait to wake up
so that this suffering can all end

i find solace in the weirdest of places
not in conversations, with people, or noise
but in the gentle quietness of nature's
blessings
as i've realized one thing
and it is that people complicate all things
instead of just appreciating the natural
current of life

child of a stolen homeland

call me crazy

but recently… i've just lost interest

in quite a lot of things

seeing the ugly side of humanity

like a storm that never calms down

has made me wonder

and taught me to let go

of all that no longer serves me

what are people waiting for

before they do something

are they waiting

for us all to disappear

and when that time comes

the only place you'll be able to visit us

would be in the pages of a history textbook

that is…

if they see us worthy of being included in

history

as history is "his story"

the story of the oppressor

and if history taught us anything

it's that it is written by the oppressor

and erases the oppressed from existence

child of a stolen homeland

i am indigenous

to the oldest land on earth

the same piece of land

that has seen wars, conquests, and famines

everyone seeks to speak about us

while denying us a voice

as they fear the native spirit

they know we have something they don't

and that ancestral spirit

is one thing

they'll never be able to break

the "free world"

is truly anything but free

as it is a prisoner

to the monster of its make-believe

supremacy

a hierarchy that never existed

but that they brought into reality

putting us into boxes

both physical and mental

they conquered and enslaved my people

but nobody bats an eye

even though our suffering is still here

child of a stolen homeland

let them think of themselves as victorious

how little they know

that they can never wipe out the originals

the natives

the indigenous ones

for every soul of ours they take

comes back to them in spirit

for generations they will never be free

as they messed with my people

and whoever messes with my people

will be condemned to suffer

for all eternity

i sit next to him, my ancestor

and i ask him questions

about his childhood on his native land

before they came and destroyed everything

for generations and we have never

recovered

he tells me: "the air was fresh

the streams crystal clear

the trees tall and strong

all our farms filled with herbs and food"

i ask him "and then?"

he looks away, wiping his tears

"and then nothing…

they came…

destroyed…

and we've been in exile ever since"

child of a stolen homeland

i can still hear their screams

the screams of my people

as they were taken from this world

and taken to the realm of the ancestors

Karim Wafa

i will never forget

how they turned a blind eye

to everything they did to us

how dare those same people

come and lecture us about freedom and

humanity

child of a stolen homeland

they call themselves the "Chosen Ones"

but chosen by who

is what i want to understand

because the last time i checked

the Lord radiates love

not hate

the Lord radiates peace

not violence

the Lord radiates justice

not injustice

so while they keep on defending their

crimes

in the name of the "One"

i've come to understand

that we do not follow the same One

they think our suffering is new

how little they know

that we are a nation of mourners

we mourn the loss of our land

we mourn the loss of our culture

we mourn the loss of our heritage

we mourn the loss of our history

we mourn the loss of our loved ones

that were taken by the greatest evil

that the world has been made to believe is

an angel

how little they know

that we are born mourners

and we die mourners

child of a stolen homeland

we do not all live the same

not at all

the air around the world

is filled with the joyful chirping of birds

whereas the air in my land

is filled with the deafening sound of bombs

people around the world

smile as they are happy to embark on new

journeys

people in my land

smile to those around them because they

know it is the end

we are not the same

my people and those of the world

we never were

and we never will be

for the people of the world

enjoy the pleasures of life

those of my land

have even their lives taken away

sometimes i close my eyes and wonder

how it was possible

for evil to masquerade as good and to have

the whole world

fall for their lies

then i remember

that the one who controls the mind

controls the world

child of a stolen homeland

an old lady from my village said
that we are the only people on earth
who are issued death certificates
before we even come into this world
as the oppressor does not even allow
our children to come into this world in
peace
they are taken from us
before being allowed to take the breath of
life

a boy from my village said

"shame on the world

shame on the ummah

where is everyone?

as you watched us perish

please do not offer us funeral prayers

it is not us that have died

it is all of you"

child of a stolen homeland

taking our ancestral land

taking the lives of my people

taking my culture and saying it is theirs

taking our history out from the history
books

so nobody in the future will ever know we
existed

but you call us the oppressor

when we cry and say "stop"

begging the world to halt our suffering

Karim Wafa

i don't understand
how they said "never again"
and yet sat by and watched
it all happening again

child of a stolen homeland

if they have taken one of us

they will take a thousand of us

if they took a thousand

who's to say they won't go to a million

is that what the world wants?

as it casually sits by

and watches us being erased

from the records of history

does it make you all happy

to see us disappearing?

one by one

soon we will all be with the ancestors

and the only voices of my people left

will be the haunting sounds of ghosts

that once were kids, mothers, fathers

but also grandparents, cousins, and friends

let the world of spirits teach you all

what happens

when you stay silent

in the face of oppression

child of a stolen homeland

oh leaders of the world

where are you?

they are all fast asleep

using our cries as lullabies

are they not ashamed?

of talking about freedom

but denying it to us

of talking about equality

but denying it to us

of talking about peace

and denying it to us

i guess all this applies

to those who only look a certain way

child of a stolen homeland

has their conscience resigned?

because how can this even be?

they destroy and cause suffering

in the night

but wake up the next morning

preaching freedom and equality

i've come to realise

that this world is a stage

as all those playing the part of angels

are nothing but demons

child of a stolen homeland

when the native is dispossessed

and the settler is given

a green light to steal

do you truly understand

that this world has lost its moral compass

the old man from my village said:

"we are the only people on earth

who pray six times a day

instead of five

because we also pray the janazah

the prayer of the dead"

child of a stolen homeland

when will they realise
that a nation who knows
that death is not the end
can never be defeated?
it will stand tall and fight
both in this world
and the next

they burn our trees

because even they know

that the trees are older

than their imaginary nation

child of a stolen homeland

they stay silent

while we're here

slowly being wiped out

what are they waiting for

to stop this?

or maybe they're just waiting

for us to perish

so that the only place

we'll be talked about

is in history classes

as they all convincingly weep

at our past suffering

and say "never again"

how little they know

that i've already heard this lie before

they wait for our bodies to become dust

and our souls to join the ancestors

before they can ever begin to admit

that they failed my people

child of a stolen homeland

no words can even begin to describe
what is being done to my nation
but what is even worse
is that no words can describe
the world's silence
as they quietly watched

maybe one day…

the future will be brighter

maybe justice will be given

who am i kidding?

they've never seen us as equals

and you expect them to start now?

child of a stolen homeland

is this what life is all about?

staying silent in the face of oppression

is one of humanity's worst vices

do they not realise?

that staying silent…

means siding with oppression

my traditions say

that in the end

even the rocks and trees will speak

and be asked to testify

and if i'm being honest

i'm eager to hear their testimony

more than any which comes out of a human

because if history has taught us anything

it's that people will stay quiet

when they need to speak up

and speak up

when that time is way overdue

child of a stolen homeland

it is the oppressor

who writes history

which is why

it comes as no surprise

that our oppression won't cease

unless our oppressor writes the truth

and for him to write the truth

he must allow us to hold the pen

are they not ashamed?

of constantly lying to the world

and expecting us all

to embrace their bitter tricks

child of a stolen homeland

the children of my land

are not just children

no

they are angels

blessing the world

but nobody sees it

as they've all been enchanted

by the forces of darkness

wake me up

when this is all over

i am tired of living a nightmare

where mankind sits by and watches

its own brothers and sisters

being ripped apart

child of a stolen homeland

they do the worst of crimes

in the name of peace

if this massacre is what they call peace

i'd hate to see what happens

when they act in the name of violence

they call it the free world

but who are they kidding

it is anything but free

it is bounded to a realm

of make-believe supremacy

a fantasy they trusted so much

that it eventually became reality

and our people

don't even get me started

they are to blame

because they walked towards the oppressor

and asked him to be their master

child of a stolen homeland

they tried putting us in chains

both mental and physical

they call themselves our saviour

while at the same time

they burned our existence to the ground

they took our rivers

then gave us a cup half full

that was used to paint them as our saviour

but their victory was short lived

because we will never submit to them

as we only bow down to our Creator

i don't want to hear anyone

ever again

talk about human rights

because if the suffering of my nation

has showed us anything

it's that human rights are only respected

when it comes to people who look a certain

way

child of a stolen homeland

i close my eyes and i see
my homeland under the shining sun
i hear the voices of laughing families
but when i open my eyes
i wonder how this is the same place
it is dark and destroyed
and the only voices heard
are those of weeping mourners

they try and wipe us out

so they can move in and rejoice

how little they know

that my people resist

both in this world

and the next

we are the ancestors

the oppressor will never have peace

he does not know

how powerful we are

when we leave this world

and turn into spirits

child of a stolen homeland

we cry

but the world does not help

it simply watches

maybe things would be different

if our tears were made of oil

how can they claim

to build a holy land

on the mass graves

of my people

the wandering souls

are not at peace

as their lands have been stolen

so they will wander around

haunting those who stole our homeland

for centuries

child of a stolen homeland

no matter how much they steal
they will never be at peace
because they are the thieves
of an ancient land and history
whose people were pushed into the world
asking for a home

when we cry

the earth cries

when we smile

the earth smiles

when we fight

the earth fights

don't you see?

you can never beat a people

who are one with nature

as we are the children of the cosmos

while our oppressor...

is the child of evil, theft and destruction

so let him have money and power

on his side

because we have the land and the ancestors

on ours

child of a stolen homeland

a soul that is indigenous

will fight for his ancestral land

until his last breath

they cut off the water supply

but the Lord unleashed

the heavenly rains

child of a stolen homeland

they were looking for a home

so we welcomed them

with open arms

we gave them the guest bedroom

suddenly

in the blink of an eye

we found ourselves in the street

the house became theirs

and we were erased from history

you took my land

my heritage

my culture

my farms

my food

my clothes

and even the souls

of my people

yet i am the oppressor?

and you are the angel?

if that is the case

then you are the angel of darkness

because i no longer know what to say

child of a stolen homeland

the women of my village

welcomed our guests

with chai

we turned our backs for a second

and our guests became our oppressors

Karim Wafa

we mourn the loss of our land

while they rejoice at our suffering

we cry over our lost souls

while they ravish in life's luxury

we do not live

we only suffer

from loss, destruction, and inhumanity

while they build their fictional nation

on the graves of my people

preventing our souls from taking a breath

please now tell me

how are they the ones who suffer?

child of a stolen homeland

my homeland

was the garden of life

it is now nothing short

of the world's largest graveyard

we suffer

and the world rejoices

how much longer can this go on?

do they not see what they are doing?

taking away lives

like a wave that brushes over the shore

their evil knows no limit

and what's worse…

is that they blame the victims for suffering

the past months have changed us all

people's true colours have been revealed

there is no longer a grey zone

you're either with oppression or against it

people i thought were good

suddenly sided with evil

and people i never expected to speak up

risked everything to fight for my nation

the world has been changed

the collective spirit of the universe has

awakened

my people are no longer alone

the world tried to bury us

but they didn't know we were seeds

now is our time to rise

child of a stolen homeland

oppression will end
the moment the world says
"enough is enough"

sometimes it all seems hopeless

but then i remember…

every single slave revolt

every single anti-colonial uprising

every single time indigenous people said

"enough"

every single time people who look like me

rose up

it all starts with a dream

to be free

child of a stolen homeland

i am tired of suffering

i just want to live

but sometimes it seems

as if that

is asking for too much

they say that they know
what it feels like
to be one of us
but do they really?
they are strangers to suffering
they live a life of fantasy
while we live a nightmare

there will come a time

when every single soul

that has been wronged

will taste

the sweetness of victory

knowing that justice has arrived

as nobody can get away

with their shrewed evilness

do they not see us as humans?

they say that they care

but actions speak louder than words

and i've come to realise

that they'll say whatever

when their soul is trying to cover up

the reality of their wickedness

child of a stolen homeland

i am done

i am tired

i am putting myself first

and this time

let the world come last

Karim Wafa

i have been deprived of freedom
for so long
that i mistook a breath of relief
as the end to my suffering

Gaza

just hearing your name

is enough to bring a million souls to tears

you have taught me

the true meaning of love

you are my everything

you have awakened something in me

that i never knew existed

you cried out to the world

and now it is the world

crying out your name in mourning

they like to preach "freedom for all"

but their actions do not mirror their words

i have learned

to not believe a word they say

they have never seen us as equals

and they definitely will not start now

child of a stolen homeland

they bombed our mosques and churches

but i could still hear

the sweet sound of prayer

amidst the destruction

that's when i knew

that those were the prayers of my ancestors

echoing from the beyond

they say that our men are barbaric

but they don't show you

how they dig under the rubble with their

bare hands

how they run to care for injured children

how they carry their mothers on their backs

how they kiss the foreheads of their stolen

fathers

how they feed the street cats before feeding

themselves

how they rock their dead daughters to

eternal sleep

how they help everyone but themselves

they dehumanized us

so you would never see us as human

child of a stolen homeland

they wiped us off
our ancestral land
and the world cheered on
thinking this is all a game

they trick you into believing
that we are anything but human
as they wipe every human
off of our native land
do you not see their lies?
when will you wake up?
you were praising the devil
who was masquerading as an angel
this entire time

child of a stolen homeland

my grandmother is a refugee

other grandmothers have the privilege

to book a plane ticket home

to see their land

my grandmother

can do no such thing

she can book a ticket

to anywhere in the world

except her home.

to see her home

all she has to do

is close her eyes

remember the past

and think of her childhood

a small boy from my land

was asked: "what would you like

to be when you grow up?"

he stared into the void for a while

and then said words so deep

they would scar humanity for centuries

he said: "i would like to be a lot of things

but i can never be anything

because we are the only children in the

world

that are never allowed to grow up

they kill us while we are young

we are born children

and we die children"

child of a stolen homeland

they say that the only place in the world

where you will forever feel safe

is on the land of your ancestors

not for me or my people

i feel safe anywhere in the world

except in my homeland

for the first time in history

the olive trees of my land

produced rotten oil

as an act of protest

against the oppressor

occupying our land

child of a stolen homeland

leaders of the world

who meet around a table

to talk about nonsense

such as peace, democracy

and human rights

forget that this very table

is made out of the bones

of my people

and it shines because

it is polished by our tears

Karim Wafa

after stealing our farms,

they wondered

why the trees stopped growing

who's going to tell them

that plants can only be fed

with water

not blood

child of a stolen homeland

a child was taken from this world

before he could ever see it

his eyes were closed before birth

and remained forever closed

this is the reality

of what it means to come from my land

not even a child

is allowed to be in peace

a dying rose

just like my nation dies

but at least the rose is allowed

to perish in peace

child of a stolen homeland

i am a child of the diaspora

my homeland is the centre to my soul

like air is central to our lungs

i may have never set foot

on my stolen nation

but it permeates through my spirit

i was prevented from kissing my native

land

but i will return

i know it

yes, i will return one day

they ask me "what's wrong?"

after having seen

the state of this hypocritical society

i answered "everything"

child of a stolen homeland

they tried to erase a people

that had become best friends with death

so nothing could scare them

as they believed in divine justice

a belief so strong

its roots were as ancient

as the roots of the olive trees

a staple in our households

is a dish called "māqluba"

a word which means "upside down"

it is cooked on the fire for hours

and then the pot is turned

it makes me think of this world

everything you were made to believe was

true

such as democracy, human rights, freedom

and equality

so-called indispensable pillars of society

are actually nowhere to be found

so in actuality

this world is "māqluba"

our olive oil has blessed

the salads of the world

under another name

our thyme has blessed

the spice blends of the world

under another name

our dates have blessed

the fruit baskets of the world

under another name

they took all native things that were ours

colonized them

and in the blink of an eye made them theirs

Karim Wafa

we are like the olive trees

they may have managed

to cut us from the land

but they forget

that our roots

are forever planted in the earth

child of a stolen homeland

i can still hear

the lullabies of my ancestors

maybe it's because

we are now closer to death

than we are to life

Karim Wafa

they bombed our land

but the Lord sent them floods

they cut our water supply

but the Lord sent us rain

they took the lives of thousands

but they came back

to haunt them as ghosts

when will they realise?

that the more they mess

with the native spirit

over time it will come back

and make them pay for their crimes

child of a stolen homeland

i was told to stay silent
because the oppressor knew
that a single word of truth
coming out of the mouth
of a native soul
was capable of shattering
the entire world
he had built on lies

Karim Wafa

my tongue was tied into a knot
to stop the flow of truth coming out of it
the sprinkled roots of trade and conquest
resonated throughout my native voice
and it was those roots of erased truth
that sent shivers down the colonizer's spine

child of a stolen homeland

i was told to never talk

about my suffering

as i had to keep

the colonizer comfortable

but by doing so

i was growing uncomfortable

so i opened my mouth

to speak the truth

and suddenly

the world woke up

Karim Wafa

i saw the suffering of my people

and i began to cry

i couldn't stop

so my tears formed a river

a river that was poisoned

by the settler colonist

who stole everything that was ours

child of a stolen homeland

we are the people of the holy land
we have been silenced for so long
that people forgot
we existed

i don't want the situation in my homeland

to make you sad

i want it to make you uncomfortable

i want it to make you furious

i want it to make you angry

i want it to move you

in a way that you have never

been moved before

let us transmute this energy into change

because change must come

this can no longer go on

we are tired

i am tired

child of a stolen homeland

they call the human race

"mankind"

but if the past two months

and 75 years

have taught us anything

it's that man

is anything but kind

they call themselves

indigenous

as they burn

our ancestral farms

to the ground

while our elders scream

"stop. please.

the trees are our children"

but the occupier

does not listen

and the world

still believes his lies.

child of a stolen homeland

we care for the land

they destroy the land

we water the plants

they burn the plants

we kiss the earth

they pillage the earth

we teach life

they teach death

i will never forget the grandfather

who kissed his dead granddaughter and said

"you are the soul of my soul"

i will never forget the small boy

who couldn't stop shaking after the bombs

i will never forget the mother

who held the body of her daughter

begging people not to take her to the

morgue

because she never liked the cold

i will never forget the baby girl

looking at a pile of hair trying to find

a strand of her mother's hair

i will not rest until every single person

who stayed silent

pays for siding on the side of evil.

child of a stolen homeland

they bomb our ruins

they destroy our shrines

they erase our history

because they are jealous

as they have none

you don't have to be muslim to feel with us

you just have to be human

you don't have to be arab to feel with us

you just have to be human

you don't have to be indigenous to feel with

us

you just have to be human

but most importantly

you need to have a heart

child of a stolen homeland

they tried to destroy our

rivers

lands

farms

plants

deserts

streams

mountains

and everything else

that our Lord had blessed us with

to convince the world that we would be

nothing

without them

the colonizer sent bombs

they took our children

and sent them to the skies

i can still hear their cries

but i can no longer answer them

they are with the ancestors now

my soul is shattered.

i miss them.

please bring them back.

please…

child of a stolen homeland

my grandmother tells me

that the ocean

carries the stories

of thousands of our people

who were taken

and never returned

Karim Wafa

we come from the land

and that is why

we have the same colour

child of a stolen homeland

my grandmother's cooking pot
carries more history
than the colonizer's kitchen

i drown

in an ocean

of my own tears

but this ocean

is not left in peace

it is poisoned by the colonizer

and all the fish that lived

thanks to my generous tears

are now dead

child of a stolen homeland

they call us barbaric

when they are the ones who turned

our skulls into cups

our bodies into bridges

our deaths into medals

our homes into theirs

our streets into graveyards

our freedom into a threat

and our nation into a wasteland

tell me again

who is the real barbaric one?

the myth of the colonizer as our saviour

exists even today

as he will set foot onto our land

act like a saint

as he is the only light man

in a nation of dark bodies

he will take pictures

of him giving us a blessing

to show the world

that we are nothing without him

but he fails to recognise

that he uses the brown and black body

as a receipt for his supremacist saviour

complex

child of a stolen homeland

our rivers flowed red

with blood

because the oppressor believed

that his freedom depended

on denying us ours

if you ever see a man

from my land

alive and breathing

appreciate it

cherish it

it is as rare as a shooting star

you might never see it again

child of a stolen homeland

they destroyed and conquered
and stole and pillaged
in the name of civilisation
but we have always been barbaric?
we are here to tell you no more
you want the truth?
i'll give it to you
we have been the civilized
you have always been uncivilized
civilize yourself
before you preach what you are not

the fuel

of racism

is the denial

of its very existence

child of a stolen homeland

they want us to forget about history
but how can we?
because this same history
is still happening today

you watch me suffer

and my nation struggling to breathe

but you do not feel with us

you have been made to believe

that we are worthless

and that our suffering is a blessing

oh just wait

because what goes around

comes around

child of a stolen homeland

i am a child of the diaspora

beaten by the world

my soul is bruised

torn apart

i am told

that i have no home

that my country does not exist

i am thrown into the ocean

and i cry

as the fish claim me

before any nation on earth has

they made us lose our land

they forced us into exile

pushed out of the only place

we ever knew to be home

we were made stateless

in our very own state

our heritage and history

our culture and identity

our people and names

all taken

by the one who claimed to come in peace

let the world know

that since the oppressor set foot on my land

we have never known peace

child of a stolen homeland

they have committed the worst of crimes
that the world ignores
they have taken thousands upon thousands
of us
yet the world ignores
they have claimed all that is not theirs
and the world yet again happily ignores
do they not realise?
that with all the violence they've inflicted
on us
they will never live in peace
at least our people both in this world and
the next
are confident and stand tall
because we are on our ancestral land
but they will never know peace
because they invaded and stole
and one day
the world will know

they are not happy people

how can they be?

if they fight and destroy just to live

whereas we love and nourish in order to

live

we are one with the Earth

the ecosystem, nature and the stars

because we were made from nature

but they came from the pits of the abyss

a place that even evil is fearful of

they want to take our homeland?

we will never give up

let us perish while we try to hold onto

whatever is left of our ancestors

because in the end

it is always the native who will win

child of a stolen homeland

we come from the Earth

we are children of the ancestors

ancestors that we want to make proud

the oppressor is trying to erase us

we will never forget who we are

despite how much they want us to

we will resist and stand tall

even if we stand alone

Karim Wafa

one day

when the sun shines bright

and the moon is full

we will speak

and our voices will be accompanied

not by the sounds of bombs or explosions

but by the sounds of nature

and the whispers of the ancestors

and that's when you'll know

that we have gained our freedom

child of a stolen homeland

i can hear the voices of my elders

when i go to the streams to collect water

i can hear the voices of my elders

when i pick olives during our autumn

harvest

i can hear the voices of my elders

when we turn the olives into oil

i can hear the voices of my elders

when the oppressor has stolen the oil

but i no longer hear my elders

once the oppressor has claimed our oil as

his

Karim Wafa

i close my eyes and imagine
a time of freedom
i wonder if we will ever be free

child of a stolen homeland

when i was a kid
i walked up to the board
and the teacher asked me
to point to my country on the map
i looked for it
searching
until i realized
that it had been wiped out
so i returned to my desk
stateless
a child of the unknown

Karim Wafa

as i close my eyes

i can hear the sounds

of our tribal drums

the nostalgic singing of our elders

but when i open my eyes

the drums are gone

and the elders are no more

i no longer recognise

this place i called home

child of a stolen homeland

i have gotten used to

not being seen as an equal

in this society which says

that it is built on equality and freedom

but can i ask one question?

equality and freedom for who exactly?

because it seems as if

my people and i are excluded from this

privilege

Karim Wafa

they say that all men are created equal

this is a statement i wish was true

but the more i hear

and the more i see

i realise that this is just a lie

a remnant of a far forgotten fantasy

because who am i kidding?

they oppressed us for centuries

they'll never see us as equals

child of a stolen homeland

they like to believe in freedom

it is only an idea

but not a reality

the world celebrates
while we mourn
the world smiles
while we cry
the world lives
while we die
you are all seen as people
but we are the only ones
who are seen as beasts

child of a stolen homeland

the world does not care for us

it never has

it does not even see us as human beings

let alone as equals

you ask me why i am furious?

how can you even ask?

do you not see?

our entire nation

can be wiped off

the face of the earth

and the world will not even bat an eye

Karim Wafa

in the future

the world will look back

child of a stolen homeland

they burn our schools, libraries and
universities
because they want us to be like them
without a history

even in the midst of all our suffering

my people find a way to smile

having lost homes, people, land, and history

we still say Alhamdulilāh (praise God)

child of a stolen homeland

they steal our land
and then claim it is theirs
i think they forgot
that if it's your land
you wouldn't colonize it

when the devil saw

what the oppressor is doing to my people

he was so ashamed of evil

that even he went back to the Lord to repent

child of a stolen homeland

i did not choose to be silent
i was purposely silenced
in a world where speaking the truth
is considered a crime

they want me to write poetry

that talks about love

happiness

and freedom

but how can i write about that

if i am denied this in my life

i do not know what love

happiness

and freedom are

because my people have had them denied

child of a stolen homeland

my nation has been destroyed

it is lifeless and grey

but there is one place

in my homeland that is still green

the graveyard

as it is watered by the tears

of our nation of mourners

they shower my people with rockets

but they forget

that there is the One who is above the

rockets

He sees and hears all

child of a stolen homeland

let me tell you about my people
we are not who you think we are
you have been made to believe
that we are evil and barbaric
to prevent you from discovering the truth
our people are as gentle as the spring breeze
our people are as kind as a mother's tender
love
our children are the purest souls you will
ever see
our women are the pillars of our nation
our men are warriors
blessed with the powers of the ancestors
our trees are ancient
going back thousands of years
our river waters flow like the love in our
souls
they told you we were evil
to prevent you from seeing who we really
are

let me tell you about my homeland

our deserts are as ancient as mankind itself

our rivers flow with crystal clear waters

our mountains rise up to touch the sky

our olive trees tell a story

that very few will ever know

our oil flows onto salads like a gentle

dressing

even thought it was made on stolen land

our oranges have blessed the kitchens of the

world

before ever reaching our own

child of a stolen homeland

they told you that our men are evil

scaring you

with our turbans and head-wraps

who speak in a foreign tongue

you struggle to comprehend

but those same men

kiss the foreheads of their children

saying the sweetest words known to

mankind

they cry out "she is the soul of my soul"

and "he is the heart of my heart"

what hurts the most

is not that we are being erased from history

it's that it is our so-called "brothers and

sisters"

that are the ones holding the eraser

child of a stolen homeland

they said that our nation was empty
what they didn't tell you
was that it was full when they arrived
but emptied over time

Karim Wafa

how ironic it is

that we live in the age of information

which interestingly has coincided

with the age of ignorance

child of a stolen homeland

he who is indigenous

will never give up

as he will stand tall

and fight for all of eternity

they tell you that we are a nation of beggars
what they don't tell you
is that when the whole world begged
we were there
and saved you all
now we need saving
none of you hear our pleas

child of a stolen homeland

we will never forget
the dad who carried the limbs
of his children in plastic bags.
we will never forget
the mother kissing the hands of children
not knowing which one was her child's.
we will never forget
the girl trying to recognise
her mom from her hair.
we will never forget.
you might forget.
we won't.

there can never be peace

on stolen land

the thief can never

become the owner

the land will reject

every foot that steps on it

which does not belong

to the descendants

of its native ancestors

child of a stolen homeland

they do not understand

how a people

as oppressed as us

are capable of resisting

for a century and going.

my grandmother says

that the native spirit

never surrenders

even if

it takes him centuries

to gain his freedom.

they want us to give up

they want us to lose hope

they want us to say it's okay

and decide to turn a blank page

but we never will forgive or forget

we will stand tall and fight for our rights

even if that means worth fighting alone

let the world know

that my nation

breathes

fights

lives

child of a stolen homeland

the olive trees

will tell a story

so traumatizing

that the world will think

it is a work of fiction

how little they'll know

that this is what the olive trees saw

and that is what the nation

of olive farmers lived through

the oppressor came and went

but we stayed rooted in the land

just like our olive trees

Karim Wafa

they look at me
and see a fearless man
someone who has everything
that is what they think
they don't know that nobody
has suffered like i have
but i stay quiet
and never speak
so i suffer in silence
while the world thinks
that i live a life of ease

child of a stolen homeland

when i raise my children
i will tell them that they come from
warriors
they are descendants of indigenous
tribesmen
that fought against the oppressor
we come from the holy land
even if the settler
tried to erase the "holy" from our "land"
i'll tell them to love their features and skin
tone
i'll tell them to embrace their tribal heritage
i'll tell them to look in the mirror
and see their ancestors staring back at them
i'll tell them that the oppressor could never
erase
the native spirit of our soul
we are here
we survived
we will live on

Karim Wafa

we will not be erased

and i will teach my children that

a nation of peace

destroyed by invading evil

child of a stolen homeland

billions around the world

celebrate the birthday of a prophet

whose homeland is being destroyed

torn apart

and reduced to rubble

if he was here today

he would expect you all to speak up

but instead of doing so

you live in a forgotten fantasy

they have for long used language
to dehumanize us
they see our lands as breeding-grounds
for division, war, strife, poverty and
suffering
forgetting that their nations are to blame
they say our lands were nothing
before they came
forgetting that our lands were lush
cradles of civilisation
they say that we were nothing
to get you all to believe
that they were everything

child of a stolen homeland

they preach life

but take the lives of our people

they say they support equality

but constantly say we are less than human

they act as if they care about us

but not only turn their backs to our

suffering

they also fund it

let them stay quiet

because their speeches about human rights

equality, freedom, and democracy

are tainted by the blood they have on their

hands

and from the hypocrisy in their souls

they call us dirty

when we taught them how to bathe

they call us ugly

when they pay to look like us

they call us uncivilized

when our lands are the cradles of

civilisation

they call our homes barren wastelands

when they are willing to risk their lives

just to set a foot on our lands

they say our nations are empty

when they cannot live without our resources

they have the audacity to talk about

humanity

when i don't see an ounce of it left in their

souls

child of a stolen homeland

innocent souls

taken from this world

far too soon

they wanted to see

the sunshine again

but the only thing

they got to see

was their life

being taken away

while the world cheered on

small kids

in their thousands

are no longer with us

because politicians could not

put an end to this madness

so thousands of loving souls

were ripped from their homes

and taken to their eternal home

in the wide-open sky

child of a stolen homeland

the world cried one word

c e a s e f i r e

but the leaders did not listen

because they preferred

the sound of cash

flowing into their hands

from the sale of cruel weapons

so they put profit above lives

and sold their souls

to the greatest of all evils

i want to write many things

but it seems as if

no words come out

my mind cannot focus

the world continues on

but i cannot accept

to go on

while my homeland

is being ripped apart

child of a stolen homeland

how much longer can this go on?
a wide erasure of one of the world's
most ancient and native people
all because those with power and money
are so eager to settle on this land
they do more than just settling
the wipe out, colonize, erase
segregate, stereotype, prejudice
alienate, oppress, and cleanse
my own people
in front of my very eyes
how can you ask me if i'm okay?
i am anything but okay

Karim Wafa

a small girl from my land

looks around her hospital room

half broken and shelled from bombings

she sees nobody she can recognise

not a single friendly face

she can only hear screams

she sees fellow patients

being rushed into this tiny place

no doctors are there

as they have all been wiped out

she closes her eyes and asks herself

"what have i done

to have been born

in the land of death

instead of the land of life?"

child of a stolen homeland

they come and steal our resources

in the name of progress

they come and steal our land

in the name of democracy

they come and erase our culture

in the name of civilisation

and they have erased our nation

in the name of peace

can the world go on like this? how can we
even live with ourselves as human beings if
we do not put an end to this madness?
sometimes it seems as if we are not all the
same because i don't understand how
someone can witness this horror and stay
quiet. how can someone feel nothing at the
suffering of others? how can people see
thousands of children being taken from this
world and sent to the world of spirits way
before their time and not feel an ache in
their souls? i don't understand. i really
don't. what has become of humanity? have
people learnt nothing? is this all a game to
them? we are talking about human lives.
people. just like me and you. do we really
want to live in a world where people do
nothing to stop this? i don't want to hear
anybody else talk about human rights,
freedom, democracy, equality, civilisation,

child of a stolen homeland

progress, evolution, and humanity ever
again. because if the erasure of my people
has shown the world anything, it's that all
these words are void of any significance in
this morally corrupted society of
materialistic and corrupted capitalist greed.

Karim Wafa

they stole our land

history, culture and identity

claiming it was theirs

now that we are furious

they want to steal our anger

and pain too

are we allowed to have anything?

child of a stolen homeland

when you want to make peace

you give an olive branch

but the settler has set

all of our native olive farms ablaze

that should show the world

that he does not care for peace

Karim Wafa

the world stands in solidarity

with our bodies

but not with our lives

child of a stolen homeland

i am a child of Gaza
i was born with a fire in my soul
probably ignited by our traditional
chilli sandwiches prepared by my granny
i am a child of Gaza
i was born with a courage in my soul
that scares even the lions of the savannah
i am a child of Gaza
i was born with an indifference to death
as my people and i
are born and die in mourning

if the world is one body

then my land is the heart

if the world is a tree

then my land is the trunk

if the world is one spirit

then my land is the soul

if the world is not of this place

then my land is paradise

child of a stolen homeland

when i walk on my land

every step i take

is followed by a prayer

uttered by the spirits

of my ancestors

but when the settler walks

on my stolen native land

every step he takes

is followed by a curse

uttered by the spirits

of my ancestors

i will never forget

those who stayed silent

child of a stolen homeland

the oppressor uses our bodies

as trophies

in the western supremacy competition

Karim Wafa

they killed our people
but our blood drained into the soil
and nourished the trees
that will live to see another century
hopefully a century when my nation
is free

child of a stolen homeland

he walks on my land
claiming it is his
while he does not speak
the language of the native
while he does not know
how to care for the land
while he does not even bother
to honor the traditions
of the people he conquered
while he erased us
from history
while he appropriated our culture
and used it as a joke
he is not from our land
he never was
and he never will be
let the whole world know the truth
because enough is enough

Karim Wafa

they say that the dead

are found in graveyards in peace

but not in my land

for the colonizer has prevented

even those who passed

from being at rest

so be careful where you walk

when you visit my land

because you'll find the dead

in the streets, rivers, mosques, churches

homes, schools, and every other place

we are a nation of martyrs

and our land has become a graveyard

child of a stolen homeland

how dystopian it is

that billions around the world

are about to celebrate the birth

of a Prophet of God

from my homeland

while that same homeland

and the people from the land

of this very Prophet

are both being wiped out

while the world remains silent

distracted by joyful songs

about this oppressed native land

the world was made to believe that we were a nation that did not exist. that we were a people that just appeared out of thin air. they believed us to be intruders. living on the land of a people that had been in exile for millennia. how little they knew. the world was tricked into believing that indigenous people were the oppressors while the settlers were the oppressed. the world was made to believe a lie so large that it led to my people being erased from history and denied our ancestral and native land. not anymore. they messed with the wrong generation. we are here. we live. we will survive. and we will make our ancestors proud.

child of a stolen homeland

it's not a war when one side is armed
and the other side is mostly made up of kids
who struggle to find food and water

Karim Wafa

oh my love

are you Palestine?

because everybody wants you

child of a stolen homeland

oh Gaza,

the world has fallen in love

with you and your people

you have taught the world

what it means to believe

even when all odds

are stacked against you

you've shown us all

that if you stand strong

for what you believe in

nobody can destroy you

the people of the world

raise a white flag

to say that they come in peace

but our people

raise white

and are still seen as threats

so the only white the world accepts on us

are the cloths of the dead that wrap our

bodies

as that is the only thing white

that the world will allow us to carry

growing up, i rarely ever talked about my
homeland. i was always told that it did not
exist and that it was a thing of the past, so i
tried to dismiss the need to talk about the
topic that was closest to my heart. it was
hard for me. but today i see that this is an
opportunity to share my story with the
world. i, like countless other indigenous
people from the holy land, have stories to
share. we were dismissed for far too long
by this society which sought to silence all
native voices in favour of white ones.
enough is enough. i remember the time a
kid my age said that they had never heard
of my homeland, and because of this, i must
have been a kid from a fictional land. they
tried to erase us from history. but we are
here. institutionalized racism and white
supremacy tried to make us a thing of the
past, confined to the history books, if we
would ever even have the privilege of being

included in history. we need to write our stories. we need to give voices to our silenced native and indigenous ancestors. we are here. i am telling their story.

child of a stolen homeland

ask yourself

why do they want to erase poets

writers

academics

professors

and other figures of art and heritage

it's because they know

that our identity

art

culture

and history

are carrier vessels

of ancient knowledge

Karim Wafa

a letter to my stolen homeland

years ago, i was sitting around my elders
and one of them spoke up one night and
said "one day in the future, the world is
going to wake up, and when it does, it will
be because of us, because of our people". i
never really gave it any thought, until the
past two months. almost a billion people
around the world are marching in our name.
millions are boycotting companies that
support the erasure of our nation. students
are calling for our freedom. i have tears in
my eyes as i write this. oh, my beautiful
Palestine, you have shown the world that
heroes do not need capes, as every single
one of our people are heroes. from the
mourning mothers and grieving
grandmothers to wounded fathers and
crying children, we are heroes for standing
up for what we believe in and fighting for

child of a stolen homeland

our indigenous rights on our native
ancestral land.
my homeland has not only awakened the
world.
it saved the world.

Karim Wafa

child of a stolen homeland

about the author

Karim Wafa, also known as Karim Wafa-Al Hussaini, is a poet, historian, writer, speaker, educator and lecturer, among other things. He has written this poetry collection in honour of his ancestral homeland, Palestine, after the start of the ongoing genocide in Gaza which began in October 2023. He is a historian of the African diaspora and the Islamic World, having given lectures around the world on a variety of topics ranging from early African American Muslims during slavery to the theological developments of various Islamic sectarian identities throughout the Medieval Muslim World. His PhD research and specialisation is on the rare presence of forgotten communities of Muslim African slaves in America before the US Civil War during the 19th century. Apart from lecturing and giving talks, he also writes and performs his poetry.

child of a stolen homeland

Printed in Great Britain
by Amazon

62212920R00153